Nancy Kozikowski
Life in Song Zhuang

This publication is based on a blog written by director Fang Li and the staff from the Song Zhuang Museum where the exhibition took place from September 2016 – February 2017.

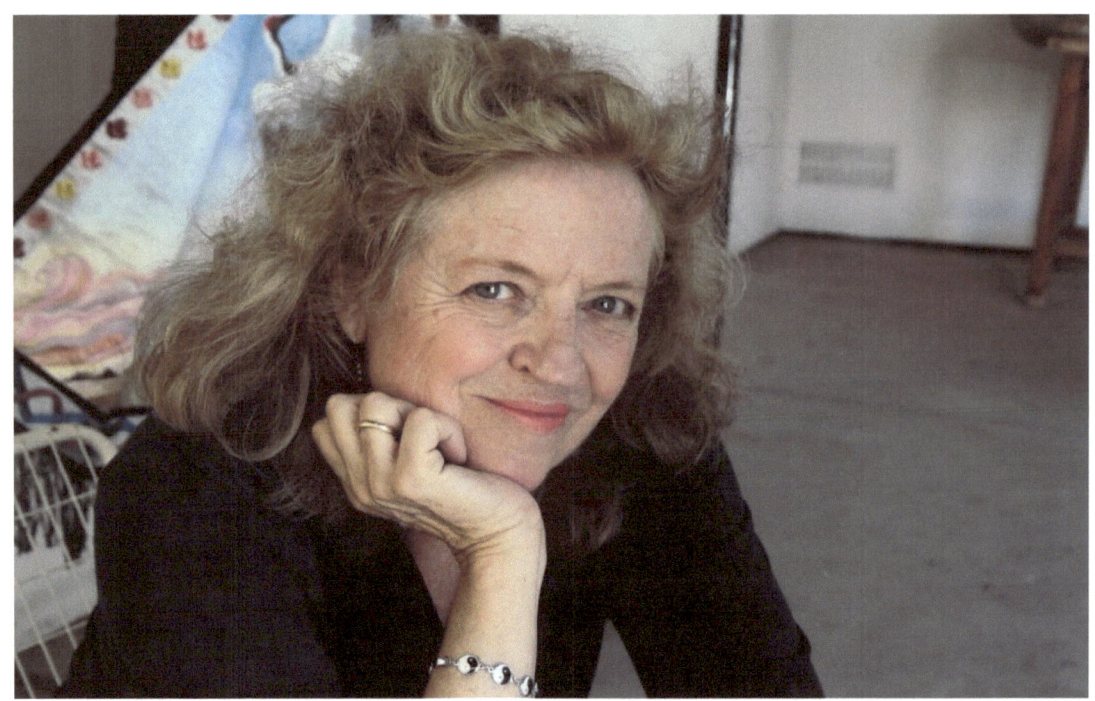

南希·柯兹考斯基

在从事了40多年的纤维艺术创作之后,我发现几何图形是可以用来表现任何事物的。我一直在尝试通过我挂毯作品来展现几何图形的魅力,并且通过颜色的深浅和流畅的图案,来展现更加立体的形象。

Nancy Kozikowski

"After 40 years of making tapestries I feel that the geometric designs which have evolved in my work express a life of their own. Working within and against the limitations of the loom and evolving from vegetable dyes to unlimited chemically dyed colors, these designs have begun to express power, movement and light.

I have tried to release the pattern from the surface of the tapestry and create a fluid, gentle, shallow and spontaneous space. I want to release the image from the medium-- into the imagination of the viewer."

- Nancy

南希的艺术经历

南希骨子里的艺术气息，**源于她的曾祖母、祖母和母**亲，她们都是艺术家。

南希发展并精炼了挂毯制作的每一道工序。从喂养绵羊、纺羊毛、收集染料植物、染羊毛毛线、设计、培训编织工，到编织挂毯并成为现在独有的Kozikowski 设计。

今天，经过Kozikowski**工作室培**训的艺术家的作品都能够看到 Kozikowski 设计直觉的影响。

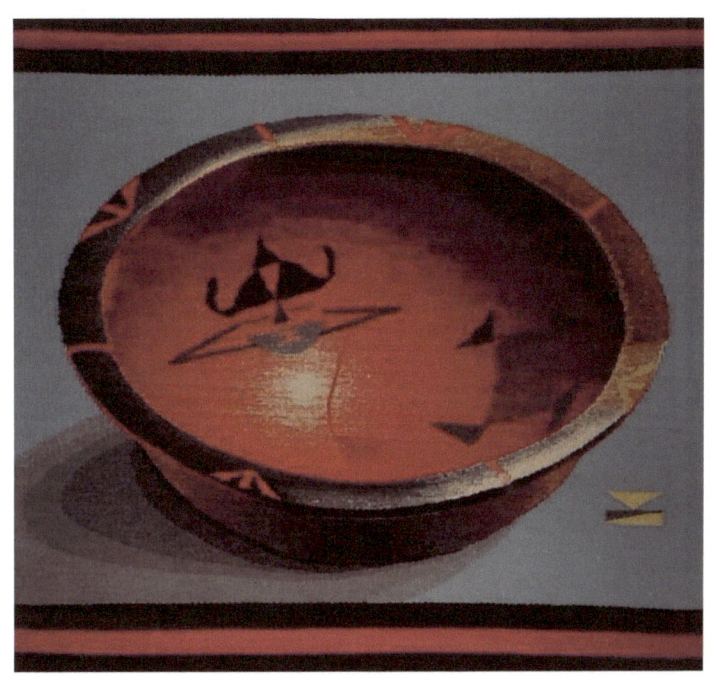

2000**年**，清华大学的挂毯设计师林乐成教授邀请南希参加"**从洛桑到北京国际纤维艺术展**"，这个艺术展汇聚了**18位新墨西哥州**纺织艺术家，这些艺术家都参加过"**新墨西哥州的线**"展览，该展览是南希1999**年**为阿布奎基博物馆组织的。

与美国三个编织工一起，南希从美国新墨西哥州来到了中国，这次行程打开了南希生活崭新的一章。受其对传统固有生活方式的兴趣所驱使，南希去了黎族和苗族聚居的村庄。南希说："他们的设计极其复杂，难度非常大，很难想象我一个人能做得出来。要好几十代的人，几百年的时间才能够完成这项工作。"

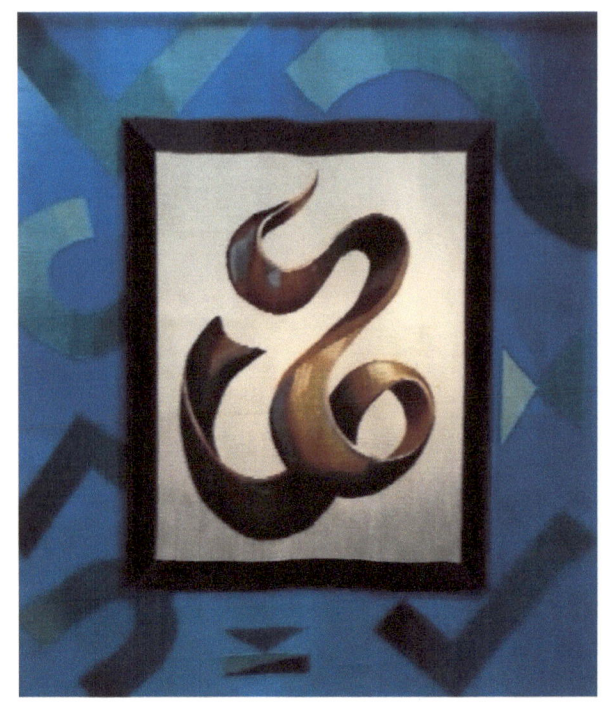

现在，南希穿梭于她位于北京宋庄的工作室和她的家乡美国新墨西哥州两地工作。

"我是一位探讨潜意识语言的当代艺术家。我把编织当作载体，因为它既是古代的，又是全球的文化"— 南希

许多公共场所都挂有南希大型的挂毯：

纽约市西奈山医疗中心

洛杉矶加利福尼亚大学的安德森（Anderson）商学院

新墨西哥州阿布奎基国际机场

科罗拉多斯普林斯市USAA 公司总部

中国北京东方广场汇贤豪庭和千禧大厦

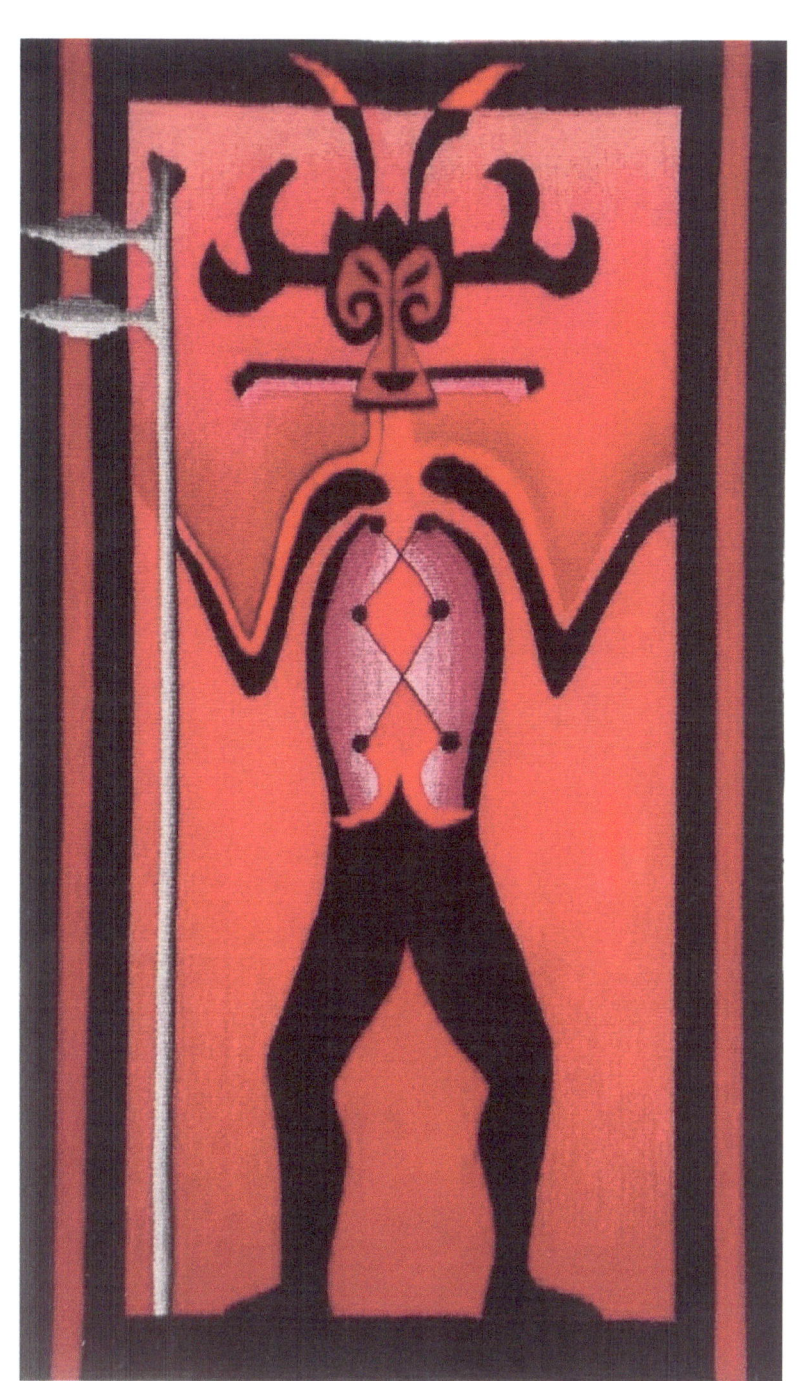

Nancy Kozikowski

Nancy Kozikowski's artistic predisposition came genetically through the traditions of her great grandmother, grandmother and mother, all of whom were artists. She developed and refined every step in the artistic tapestry process. From raising sheep, spinning wool, building looms, gathering dye plants, dying the wool, creating designs, training weavers, and weaving the tapestries into what is now distinctively known as Kozikowski Design.

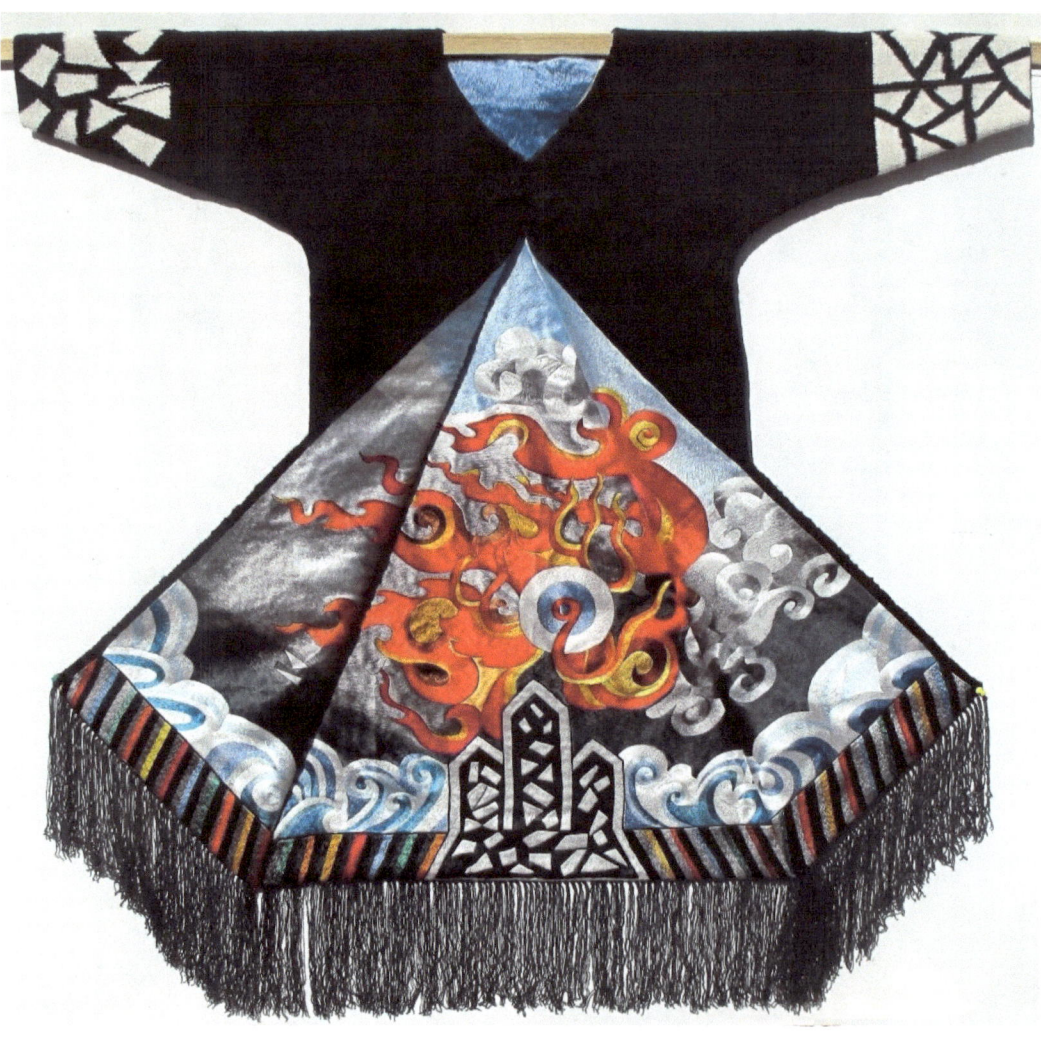

The influence of Kozikowski design sensibilities is seen today in the works of those artists who have trained at Kozikowski Studios.

In 2000, Professor and tapestry designer, Lin LeCheng, from Tsinghua Academy invited Nancy to participate in "From Lausanne to Beijing International Fiber Art Exhibition". This exhibition included eighteen New Mexican textile artists from the "Thread of New Mexico" exhibition which Nancy curated for the Museum of Albuquerque in 1999.

Accompanied by three native weavers from the USA, Nancy traveled from New Mexico to China. This opened a new chapter in her life. Motivated by her interest in indigenous traditional lifestyles, she traveled to villages where the Li people and the Miao people live. "Their designs are extremely complex and profoundly difficult. I can't imagine doing them myself. It takes many generations or hundreds of years to be able to do this work." said Nancy.

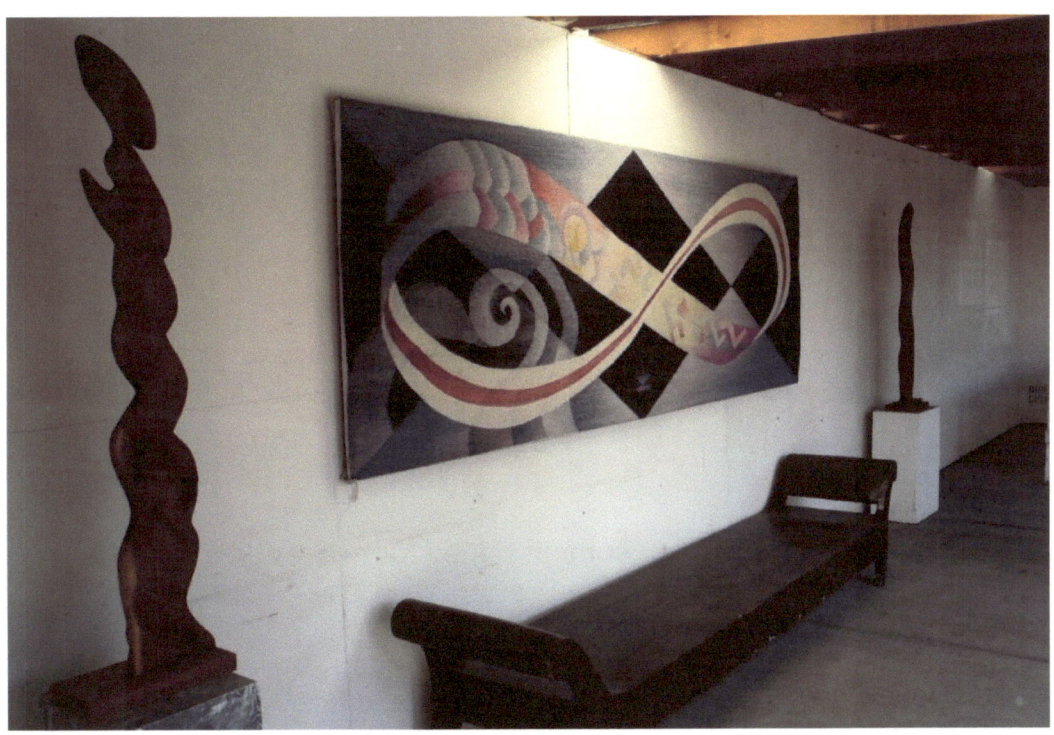

Currently Nancy works from her studios in the artist village of SongZhuang, near Beijing, and in her home town of Albuquerque, New Mexico, USA.

"I am a contemporary artist exploring subconscious language. I have chosen weaving as my medium because it is culturally universal and ancient. My real love is to explore subconscious communication through art and time. "

-Nancy

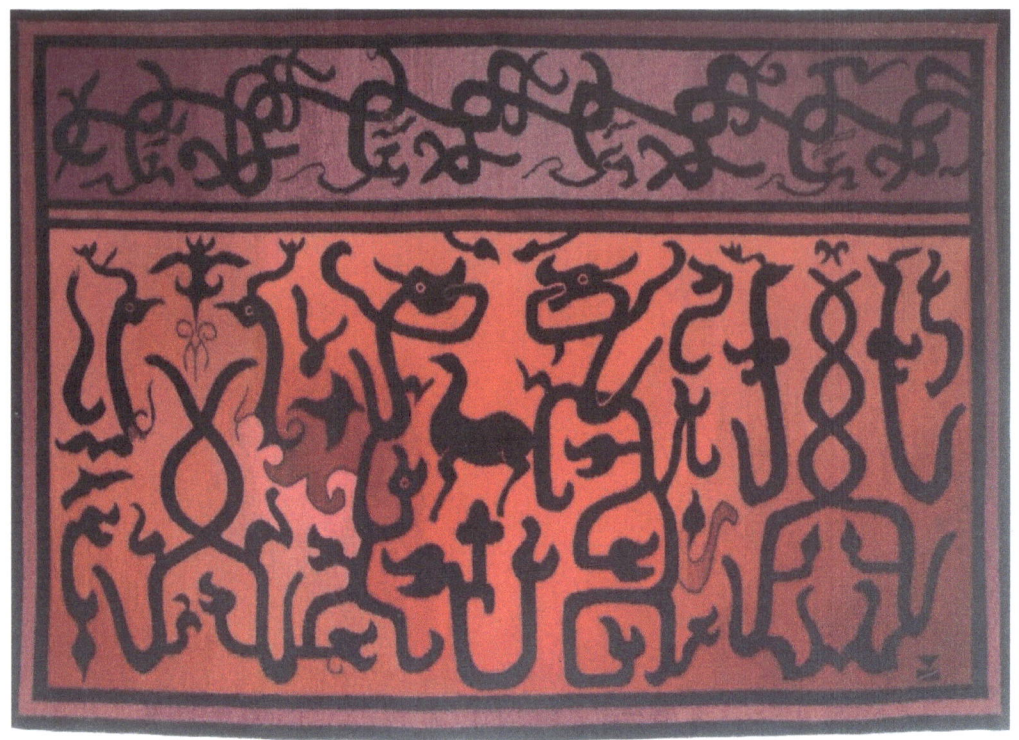

Nancy's large tapestries have been commissioned for many public spaces including:

Mount Sinai Medical Center, New York City, New York,

Anderson Business School at University of California at Los Angeles,(UCLA)

Albuquerque International Airport, Albuquerque New Mexico,

USAA Corporate Headquarters, Colorado Springs, Colorado.

Millennium and Centennial Towers at Oriental Plaza, Beijing, China,

NK in SongZhuang

"In 2007 I was invited to participate in the International Artist part of The SongZhuang Art Festival.

I brought a loom and invited visitors to the festival to weave an inch. This gave participants an opportunity to experience the process of weaving.

I believe that everyone in the world had great, great grandparents, before the industrial revolution, who were involved in or were aware of some aspect of raising silk, sheep, flax or cotton, spinning, dyeing or weaving. These are now esoteric skills. I only 15 years ago found out that my great grandfather was a weaver in Germany before he came to America."

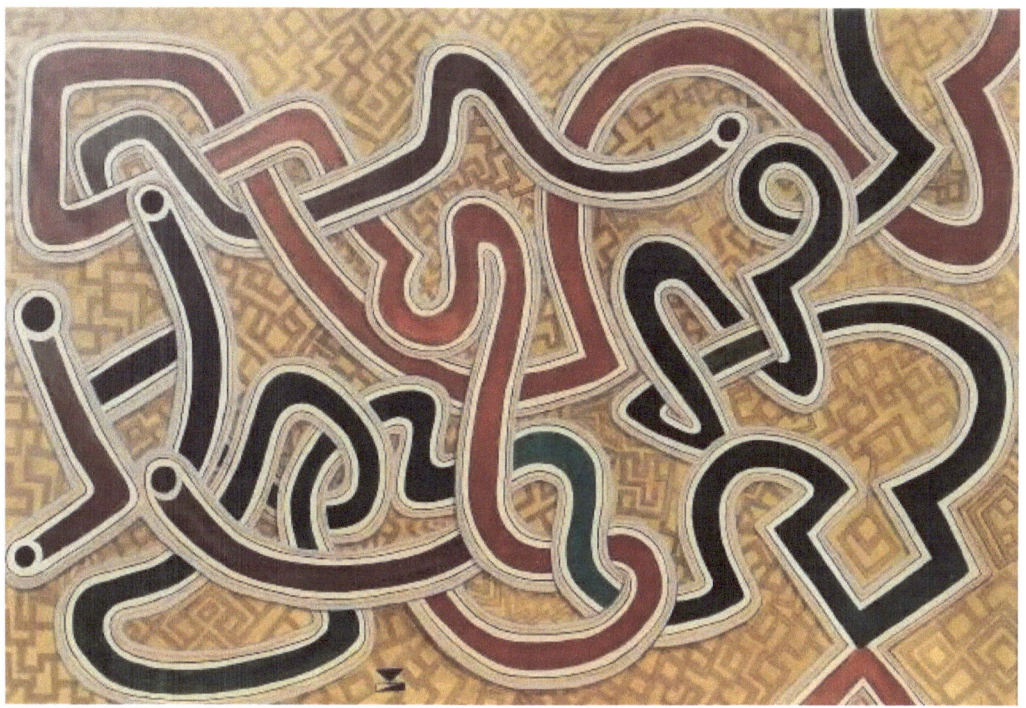

"I fell in love with SongZhuang. I asked my husband why I love this place so much. He said, 'Because it's like Medanales'. For 12 years I lived in Medanales, a small village in Northern New Mexico, USA. It's true, I do love living in a village. A village is a village whether in New Mexico or China. My definition of a village is a self-sufficient, self-centered, quiet place that has been lived in for a long time."

- Nancy

During the SongZhuang Festival Afeng found me in our exhibition space. I had met Afeng seven years before at Tsinghua University during my first trip to China. She took me on her motorbike to her studio. She had a picture of us together from 2000. She encouraged me and helped me find a studio to rent in XiaoPu. I am very grateful for this coincidence and Afeng's friendship."

- Nancy

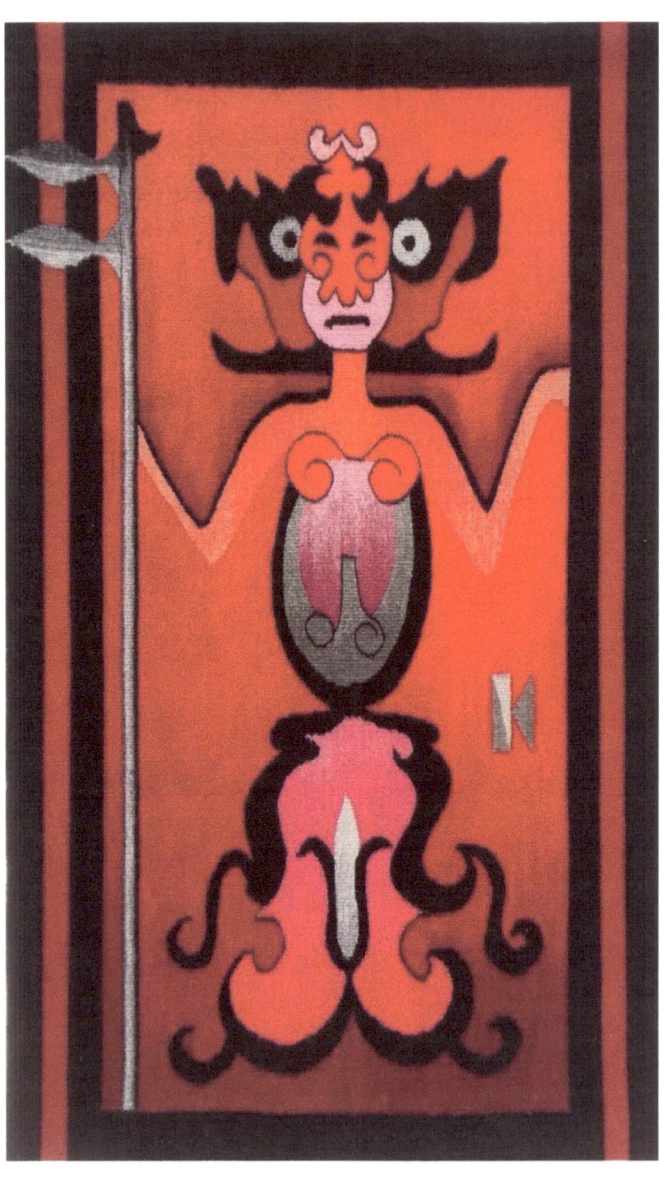

"During the 2007 Festival the Song Zhuang Museum opened. It's a beautiful museum, under the direction of Li Sheu Fang.

To help me with the 2007 Festival project I met LuXiangRu. She is a spectacular weaver and person. She has been living and working with us ever since. She didn't speak English and my Chinese is terrible but we both understand weaving, cooking, family, gardening. We study our languages together. Wo men hu xiang xue xi. The best of possible worlds.

For the first two years I was here I had two projects that kept me busy. One was to make six – 3m X 4m tapestries for an Indian casino and hotel in Albuquerque, New Mexico, my home town. This included developing the designs, weaving mockups, as well as the final designs. The other job was to write and illustrate a small book on the process of weaving tapestry for a class I was teaching at Gong yi mei shu da xue in JiaDing near Shanghai.

For the first few years I lived in XiaoPu during the week and spent weekends with my husband John in Beijing.

Because my mother was in her 90's I needed to return to New Mexico to be with her. So our schedule has been three months in China and three months in the US and so on for the last eight years. My mother died last month so my schedule may change. Recently John has moved to the Village.

I do big public commissions. Between commissions I do smaller pieces for sale and for shows.

I love our HuTong/ courtyard studio. Zhi Nu Gong Zhou Shi. There is a beautiful, traditional painting on the eves and a tile roof. The southern exposure warms the studio in the winter. But it needs insulation."

- Nancy

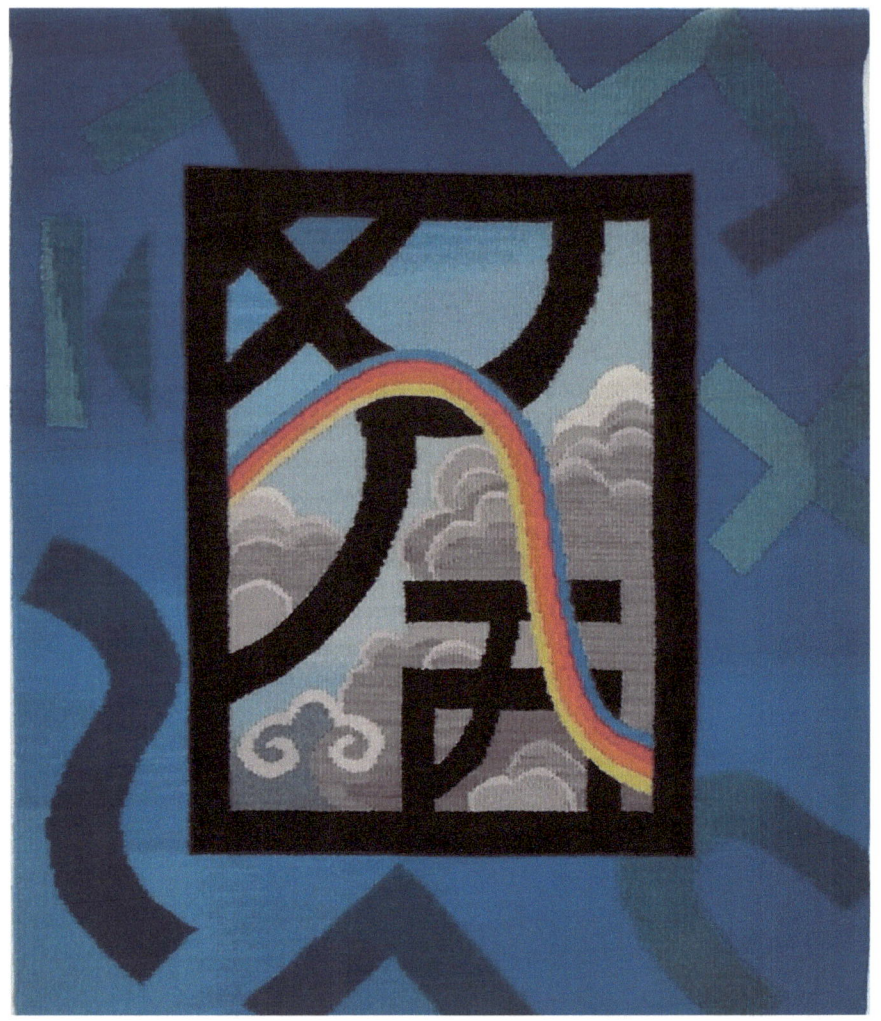

"I have heard that my studio in XiaoPu will be torn down in five years. This will be a shame. I'm from New Mexico. Santa Fe, the Capital of New Mexico, is considered the second most successful art market in the US. The reason this small town is so popular is because it has preserved the traditional adobe architecture and diverse old culture. Santa Fe is like SongZhuang in that so many artists live and work there, both places have many galleries and museums. In Santa Fe there are traditional Indian and Spanish artists along with contemporary Artists. This huge variety of styles and cultures gives it an appeal to everyone, like SongZhuang. Preserving cultural roots is an art form. SongZhuang is already a ready-made art center but if the cultural architecture is destroyed it will be just another TongZhou. I hate to see the loss of the roots of a natural resource, especially in an 'Art Center' - Save XiaoPu!!"

- Nancy

"Last year for the SongZhuang Festival I saw one of the best shows I've ever seen. It was the show called "We". It included more than 700 self-portraits of artists from SongZhuang. The variety of styles and expressions was awesome. I wanted to sneak in and add my self-portrait to the show.

At the same time the Shang Shang Museum's show of over 1000 pieces was spectacular. I've been here long enough to see the museum become more refined and artists evolve. World class! This place is heaven for an artist. One is surrounded by inspiration and art supply stores. Who could ask for anything more? Oh yes, customers."

- Nancy

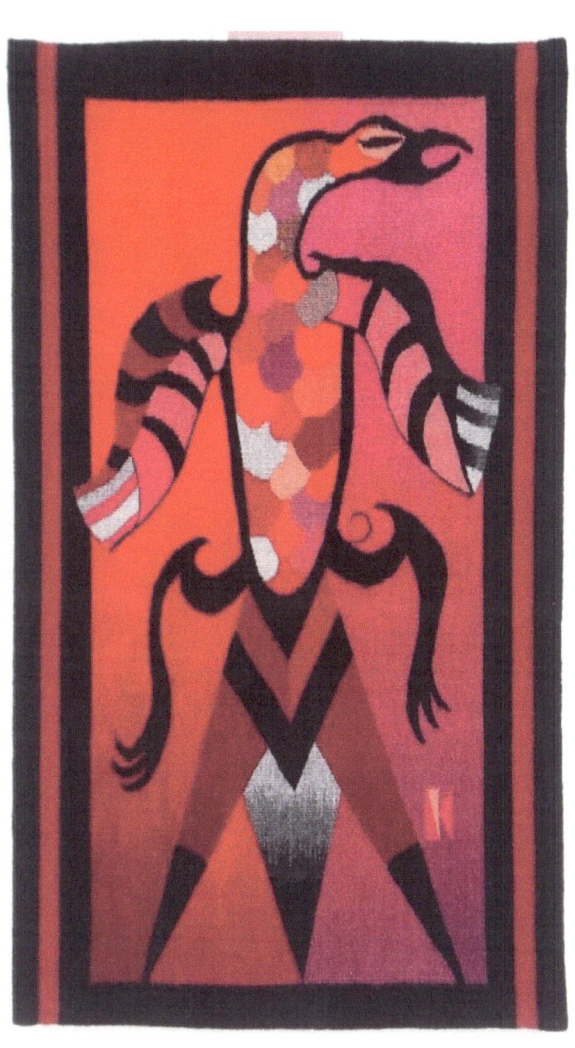

"It seems that many people from Beijing have heard of SongZhuang but few have visited. I believe Beijingers need someone to show them the way. Every day there are more wonderful restaurants here. Maybe a phone app with lists of museums, galleries, restaurants, hours, and maps would help.

I am so happy to live and work here. And I am very grateful to be included in this exhibition. Maybe I will include my self-portrait in the show."

- Nancy

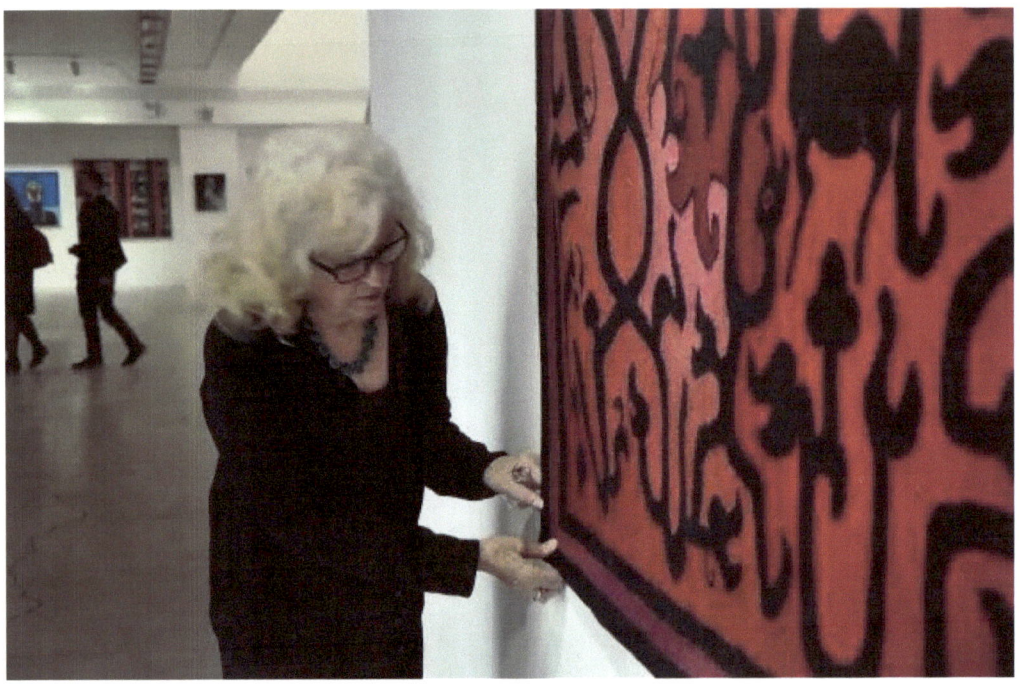

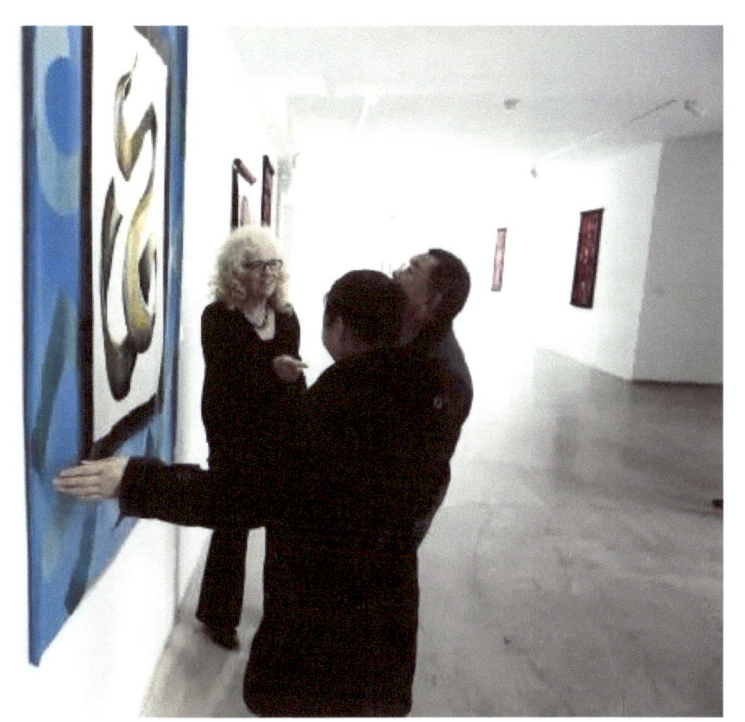

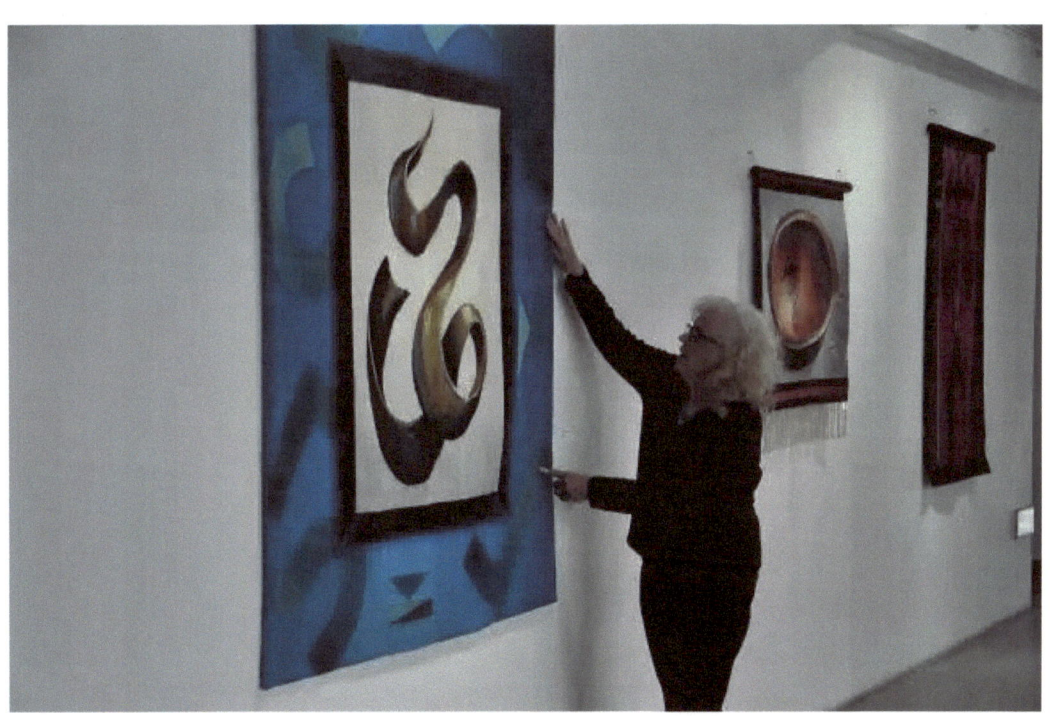

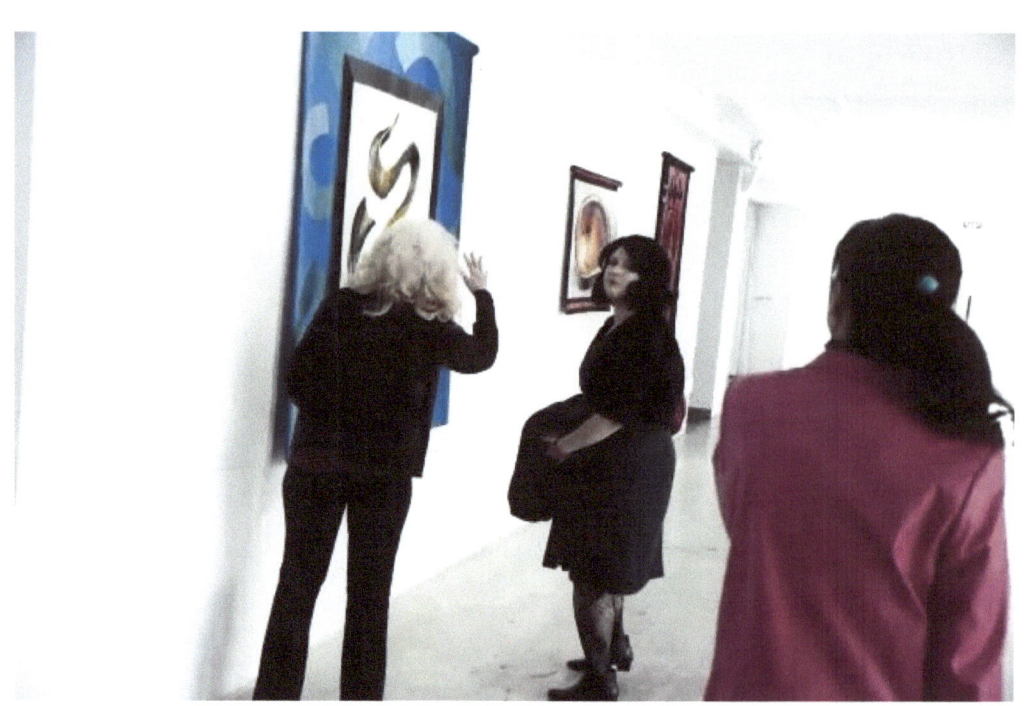
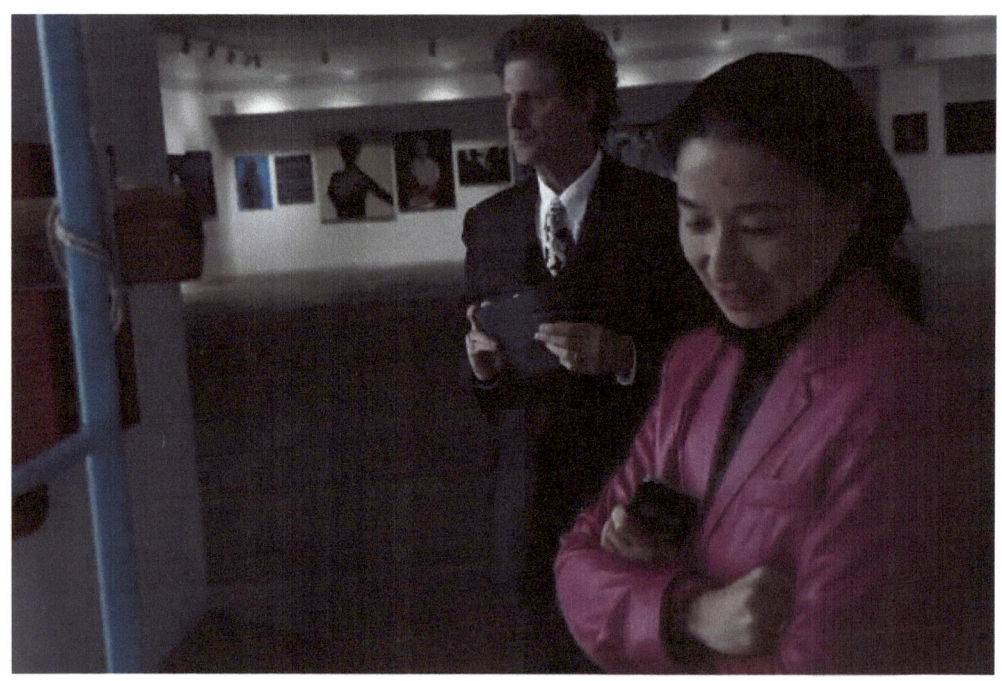

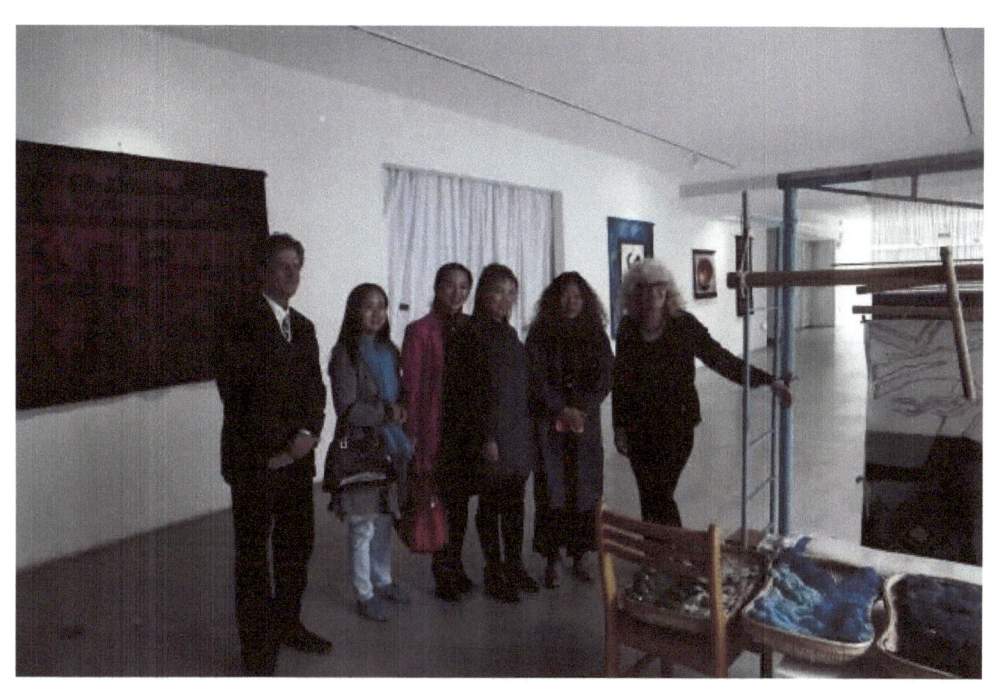
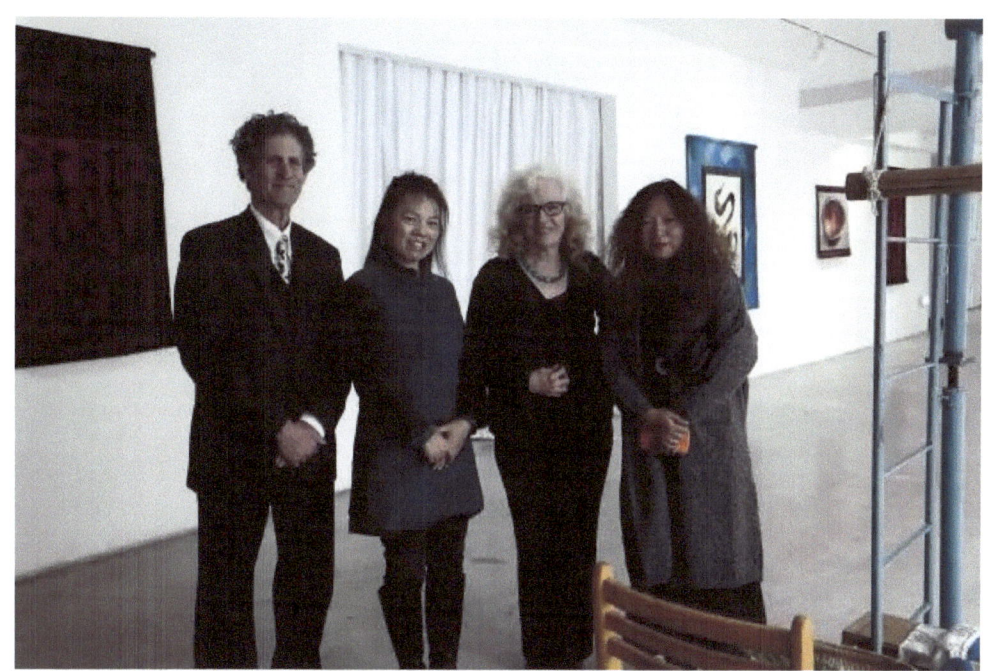

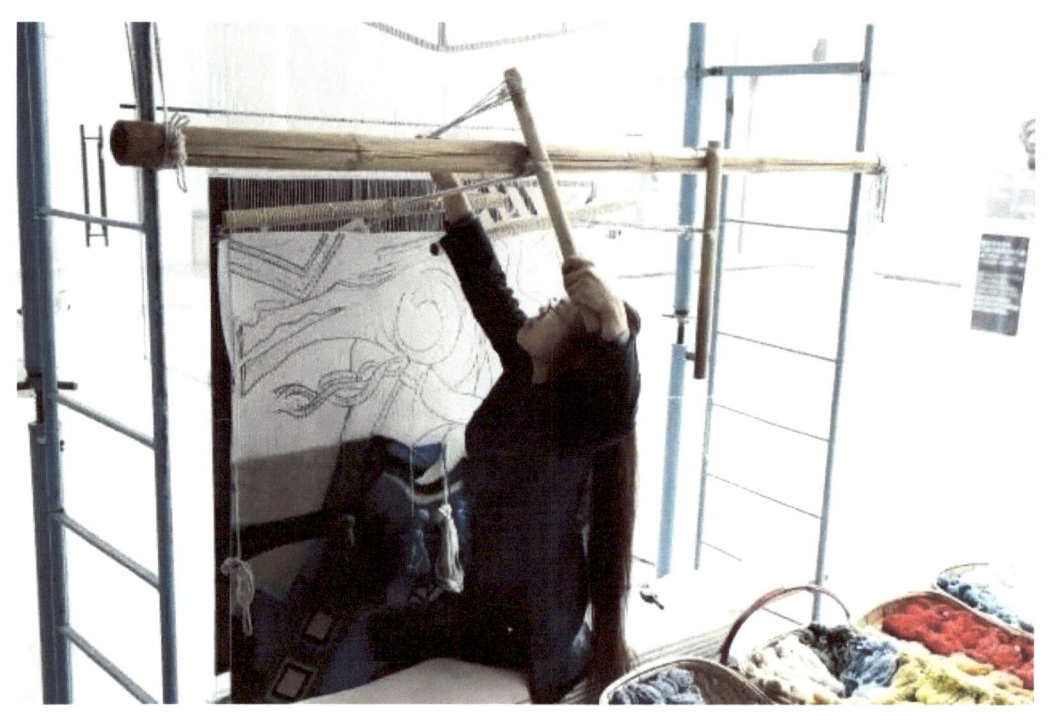

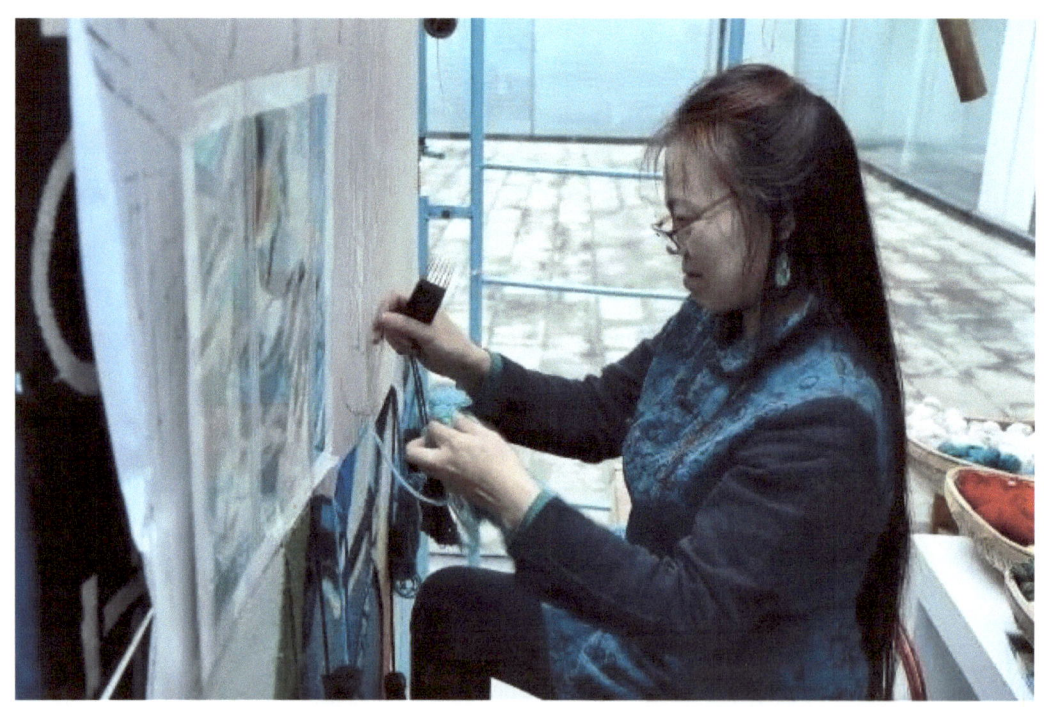

展览

2015 经纬中西——编织连接世界，林乐成和南希，阿布奎基博物馆和DSG Fine Art艺术馆，美国新墨西哥州，阿布奎基市。

2015 经纬中西——编织连接世界，林乐成和南希，沈阳大学，沈阳市

2015 经纬中西——编织连接世界，林乐成和南希，鲁迅艺术学院，沈阳市

2015 经纬中西——编织连接世界，林乐成和南希，长春大学，长春市

2014 南希挂毯和油画新作品展，美国新墨西哥州，阿布奎基市

2012 1895 传统的演变艺术展，江苏省

2012 南希作品个人展，上上美术馆，北京宋庄

2010 南希和苏珊的新作品展，DSG Fine Art艺术馆，美国新墨西哥州，阿布奎基市

2008 南希个人作品展，北京宋庄，韩燕画廊

1992 南希个人作品展，美国纽约市，卡乔拉美术馆

1990 瓜达鲁普历史博物馆，美国新墨西哥州，圣达菲市

1989 西南部的编制艺术，南希和亚努什，美国新墨西哥州，陶斯市

1988 American Business Interiors, Albuquerque, NM 公司

1986 罗伯特·富尔美术馆，法国巴黎

1985 羊仓画廊，美国新墨西哥州，阿布奎基市

1983 十号美术馆，美国纽约

1983 圣约翰教堂，美国纽约

1982 后尚美术馆，美国德克萨斯州，达拉斯市

1982 因西欧斯美术馆，美国新墨西哥州，圣达菲市

1981 开铃艺术馆，美国加州，萨克拉门托市

1981 圣达菲美术馆，美国新墨西哥州，圣达菲市

1980 蝴蝶美术馆，美国新墨西哥州，阿布奎基市

1979 萨皮塞克艺术馆，波兰，华沙市

1978 粘土与纤维艺术馆，美国新墨西哥州，陶斯市

1975 伊莱恩艺术馆，美国新墨西哥州，圣达菲市

1974 当代民间艺术馆，美国加州，洛杉矶市

1974 希尔艺术馆，美国新墨西哥州，圣达菲市

1974 伊莱恩艺术馆，美国新墨西哥州，圣达菲市

1974 蝴蝶美术馆，美国新墨西哥州，阿布奎基市

1973 伊莱恩艺术馆，美国新墨西哥州，圣达菲市

1973 希尔艺术馆，美国新墨西哥州，圣达菲市

Exhibitions

2015 Albuquerque Museum and DSG Fine Art, Albuquerque, New Mexico, China: East West Warp Weft: Weaving Connects the World: Lin Le Cheng and Nancy Kozikowski

2015 Shenyang University, Shenyang, China: East West Warp Weft: Weaving Connects the World: Lin Le Cheng and Nancy Kozikowski

2015 Lu Xun Academy, Shenyang, China: East West Warp Weft: Weaving Connects the World: Lin Le Cheng and Nancy Kozikowski

2015 ChangChun University, Changchun, China: East West Warp Weft: Weaving Connects the World: Lin Le Cheng and Nancy Kozikowski

2014 Jia Sheng Culture Media Women's Art Festival, Zhalainuoer Museum, Manzhouli, China (Artists Representative Speaker)

2013 Song Zhuang Art Festival Invitational Sunshine Museum, Song Zhuang, China

2013 Blow Up Your Mind Rodin International Gallery - Songzhuang Xiaopu, China

2013 Not Strangers International Artists Invitational, Huan Dao Museum, Song Zhunag, China

2013 Juried Invitational (Juror) Da He Wan (Gulf) Museum, Song Zhuang, China

2013 KIAF Korean International Art Fair, Seoul, Korea

2013 Jeon Ju Invitational Exhibition, Jeon Ju Korea

2013 Song Collection Tour of One Hundred Artists in Kubuq, Inner Mongolia (catalogue page 134)

2012 Lausanne to Beijing 7th International Fiber Art Biennale (Juror) Nantong China

2012 4th International Tour Show (Park Fine Art) Song Zhuang, China, Seoul Korea, Istanbul, Turkey, Albuquerque, NewMexico, USA

2012 KIAF Korean International Art Fair, Seoul, Korea

2012 The Evolution Of Tradition, Exhibition, Lecture, Workshop, JeonJu, Korea

2011 The Cross Yinna Yang Art Center, Songzhuang, Tongzhou, Beijing

2010 Textile Connections, Tokyo University of Arts, Japan

2010 Lausanne to Beijing 6th International Fiber Art Biennale (Juror)Zheng Zhou, Henan,

2008 Lausanne to Beijing 5th International Fiber Art Biennale (Juror)

2008 Han Yan Gallery Song Zhuang Live Draw

2007 Song Zhuang Art Festival International Art Exhibition Invitational

2006 From Lausanne to Beijing 2006 4th International Fiber Art Biennale (Souzhou) (Catalogue page 137)

2006 China Yunan International Folk Arts and Crafts High-Level Forum

At Yunan Provincial Museum and Yunan Provincial Library Kunming China

2004 "From Lausanne to Beijing, Suzhou 3rd International Tapestry Art Exhibition"

2003 "Live Draw" DCA, Venice CA

2003 "Abstract Art" Anderson Contemporary, Santa Fe, NM

2003 "Live Draw" Dartmouth Street Gallery, Albuquerque, NM

2003 "New Mexico in Kansas" Rice Gallery, Overland Park, KS

2002 "From Lausanne to Beijing -Shanghai 2nd International Tapestry Art Exhibition"

2001 "Thread of New Mexico" (created by Nancy Kozikowski) Albuquerque Museum, Albuquerque NM

2001 "Nancy Kozikowski Invites II" Dartmouth Street Gallery, Albuquerque, NM

2000 "From Lausanne to Beijing—Beijing 2000 International Tapestry Art Exhibition"

1999 "Nancy Kozikowski Invites" Dartmouth Street Gallery, Albuquerque, NM

1997 "Rock Scissors Paper" , Anderson Contemporary Arts, Albuquerque, NM

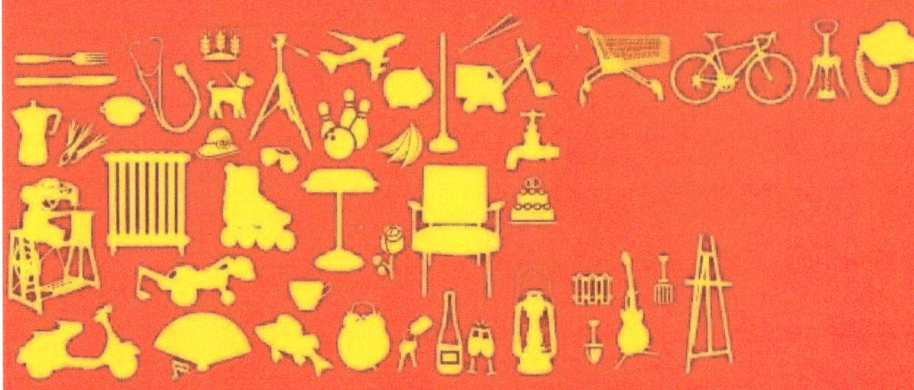

生活在宋莊
[国际版] INTERNATIONAL
LIFE IN SONG ZHUANG

2015 — 2016
10.24 – 02.24

策展人：方蕾 Curator: Fang Lei

参展艺术家 Participating Artists

Alex Santate · Alvaro · Andrew Crooks · Bharat Singh & Gurinder · Brendan A. Knape · Cristobal Ortega · Daniel Moussier · Denise Keele-bedford · Gisela · Hero · Johannes Nielsen · Kohl & Layton · Ludovic De Vita · Marc Baurière · Nancy Kozikowski · Nick Perret · Nicola · Tine

主办：宋庄美术馆　　　Organizer: Song Zhuang Art Center
特别主办：雪景成（北京）文化艺术有限公司　Special Organizer: Snowscape Culture and Art (Beijing) Co., Ltd.

鸣谢 Thanks
北京市北亚景观规划设计有限公司 Beijing Zalk Landscape Planning Co., Ltd.
京家家居设计（上海）有限公司 Ritz Design Co., Ltd.
泰禾泉水俱乐部 Placid Rivers Club

http://weibo.com/songzhuangartcenter　　www.sz-artcenter.com

生活在宋庄【国际版】

策展人：方蕾

Curator : Fang Lei

参展艺术家：

Participating Artists :

Alex Santate 阿列克斯·赛塔非【西班牙】

Alvaro 阿里巴鲁【西班牙】

Andrew Crooks 安德鲁·库克斯【美国】

Bharat Singh & Gurjinder 印度兄妹/巴拉特&丽金【印度】

Brendan A. Linane 布伦丹·利纳内【英国】

Cristobal Ortega 多巴【西班牙】

Daniel Moussier 丹尼尔【法国】

Denise Keele-bedford 德妮丝【澳大利亚】

Gisela 吉塞娜【西班牙】

Heini 艾尼【瑞士】

Johannes Nielsen 汉森【瑞典】

Kuhl & Leyton 库尔&雷顿【美国】

Ludovic De Vita 帅多维克·德·维塔【法国】

Marc Baufrère 马克【法国】

Nancy Kozikowski 南希·柯兹考斯基【美国】

Nick Perret 尼克·佩里【瑞士】

Nicolai 尼古莱宋【冰岛】

孙东俊【韩国】

Tine Deturck 迪娜·德杜柯【比利时】

展览时间：2015.10.24-2016.02.24

Duration：Oct24th,2015-Feb24th,2016

开幕时间：2015年10月24日 15:00

Opening：Oct24th,2015

展览地点：宋庄美术馆

Venue：Songzhuang Art Center

主办：宋庄美术馆

Organizer :Song Zhuang Art Center

特别主办：雪景观（北京）文化艺术有限公司

Special Organizer :Snowscape Culture and Art (Beijing)Co., Ltd.

鸣谢 Thanks：

北京佐克园林景观规划设计有限公司

Beijing Zalk Landscape Planning LTD.

丽兹家居设计（上海）有限公司

Ritz Design Co., Ltd.

泰禾商务俱乐部

Placid Rivers Club

行车路线：

【公交】大北窑桥下乘808或809宋庄美术馆下

Public Transport:Bus808 809,dabeiyao-songzhuang Art Center

【自驾】大北窑上通燕高速到宋庄出口往北到小堡村宋庄美术馆

Traffic Route:Dabeiyao-Yan-tong Highway-Exit Songzhuang Art Center

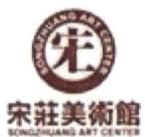

宋庄美术馆官方网站

http://sz-artcenter.com

宋庄美术馆官方微博

010-89579897

宋庄美术馆公共邮箱

songartcenter@126.com

全面合作伙伴：雪景观ART

www.dsg-art.com
www.kozikowskidesign.com
www.nancykozikowski.com

www.ingramcontent.com/pod-product-compliance
Lightning Source LLC
Chambersburg PA
CBHW051825210526
45473CB00005B/1741